P9-DFQ-705

ROTTEN REVIEWS REDUX

ROTTEN
REVIEWS
REDUX

A·LITERARY·COMPANION

PUSHCART

EDITED BY BILL HENDERSON

**INTRODUCTION BY ANTHONY BRANDT
ILLUSTRATIONS BY MARY KORNBLUM**

ISBN 978-1888889-68-0
Pushcart Press, P.O. Box 380, Wainscott, NY 11975

Distributed by WW Norton Co.

For Walt Whitman,
who may have written
some of his best reviews
himself.

Why Rotten Reviews Redux?

Twenty-five years ago, when the first edition of this slim satire was published by Pushcart Press, a certain literary civility prevailed. Even so, now and then, an explosive bit of gratuitous vitriol escaped. Sometimes, as Kurt Vonnegut put it, "preposterous loathing" inflamed the reviewing page.

Such loathing is no longer rare in the glorified age of the Internet. In fact, this marvelous digital tool, far from bringing us closer together, has induced a state of almost perpetual warfare on-line, in print, in politics, on talk shows. We've entered the century of unfettered, unedited, unfiltered, and ridiculous rage.

What's worse, today's rotten reviews are often anonymous. A quarter century ago, in the innocent days of our first edition, an anonymous put-down was the mark of a coward. If you couldn't sign your real name to a remark, it was dismissed, and you were too, whoever you were.

No longer. Anonymous on-line critics ambush unprotected writers in bursts of verbal automatic rifle fire.

I, who happily own no computer and was unaware of such practices, was deprived of my innocence when a little, otherwise well appreciated memoir I wrote was "reviewed" on-line. The book was ignored. I wasn't. An "old fool" I was branded. No real name of the so-called critic. No address. A rotten review had become personal.

I realized that now we live in an on-line Wild West. All civility gone. Empathy, balance, decency, knowledge, out the window. Everybody a blogger. Everybody an instant critic.

Redux time.

The first Rotten Reviews *was inspired by a few such attacks, pre-internet, on books I had published at Pushcart Press, books that I loved, by writers I respected. My revenge daydream then was to pay a visit to the office of the reviewing organ and break pencils. I mean these books had taken the authors years to compose, sometimes a lifetime. And to have them dismissed so casually, well . . . it just wasn't fair. Instead of mayhem, I chose mockery. Thus,* Rotten Reviews, *a surprise best seller in its day.*

Beware contemporary rotten reviewers, the original Rotten Reviews *is back. More to come. Your thoughtless chatter may live in immortality, as does the rot that follows. The joke may be on you.*

BILL HENDERSON

This book is for all writers who spent years, if not a lifetime, writing a book and then had it dismissed by a rotten review.

Rotten reviews have happened to some of the best books and authors, and here are a few of them, with their detractors.

In determining the best books and authors I let history have the final say. Each of these books has lasted for at least twenty-five years—a publication date of 1961 was our cut-off—and some have been respected for centuries. Under the heading of Review, I have included not only periodical reviews but critical essays, diary entries, letters and reported conversation.

While researching this modest survey, I was impressed by the balance, intelligence and fairness of most reviewers. The truly malicious review was a rarity.

Often reviewers went into spasms of appreciation for books of slight value: "Martin Tupper (1810-1889) has won for himself the vacant throne waiting for him amidst the immortals, and has been adopted by the suffrage of mankind and the final decrees of publishers into the same rank with Wordsworth, Tennyson and Browning." The Spectator *(1866)*

Even bad reviews were appreciated. When the Concord Massachusetts public library banned Huckleberry Finn, *Mark Twain exulted : "That will sell 25,000 books for sure!"*

Rotten Reviews *is not a scholarly study. When available I have quoted from the original documents, but often review digests, critical text editions and biographies were the source of the bad blurb. In each case, the opinion cited appeared about the time of the book's publication, unless otherwise noted. I have concentrated on English, European and American literature, which leaves out a whole world of ill-will from other countries.*

BILL HENDERSON

It is safer to assume that every writer has read every word of every review, and will never forgive you.

JOHN LEONARD

A couple of years ago I was asked to review a minor work by a well-known writer, and, after some hesitation, accepted the assignment. I hesitated because, although I did not know the writer, we shared a friend, a man I shall call Don; and Don was passionately committed to this woman's work and thought her without parallel among contemporary novelists. Suppose I didn't like the book? How would Don react? Don and I weren't close but I did respect him. I thought he was a better writer, in fact, than his esteemed lady friend, and I didn't particularly want to alienate him for the sake of such a slender, inconsequential thing as a book review.

Nevertheless I took the assignment, the book came in the mail, it turned out to be dreadful, insensitive and superficial in the extreme, and I swallowed hard and gave it a rotten review. A few weeks later, shortly after the review had appeared, I walked into the local bar where both Don and I hang out; there was Don, sitting at a table with some friends. I went over to say hello and he gave me a long, hard stare. "Ah," he said finally, "it's the Reviewer." He hasn't spoken to me since.

I got off easy, of course. One friend lost is nothing. Other Reviewers lose whole continents of friends. Still others get anonymous threats in the mail. There have been cases of actual physical assault; one irate author threw a Reviewer I know down a flight of stairs. All are regularly subject to long letters impugning their intelligence, their integrity, their humanity, which letters appear

13

in the very publications that employ them. And for what? Reviewing will never make one rich. The enemies one makes writing reviews will almost inevitably seek revenge if one should be so foolish as to publish one's own books. And one may very well wind up someday immortalized in sly little anthologies like this, egg permanently smeared all over one's face, because one thought a minor work by a well-known writer was insensitive and superficial in the extreme and it has turned out to be—who could have guessed it?—a classic.

It is enough to give one pause. It is enough, indeed, to incline one to abandon reviewing altogether. Who would want to have called *Wuthering Heights*, not too long after it had appeared, "a crude and morbid story," or to have said about Dickens and one of his greatest novels, *Our Mutual Friend*, that "We are convinced that it is one of the chief conditions of his genius not to see beneath the surface of things. . . . We are aware that this definition confines him to an inferior rank."? That it was Henry James who made these remarks only reinforces the point. If great writers can be wrong about other great writers, how do mere Reviewers summon the nerve to pass judgments? One of the pleasures of this wicked collection is watching the great being terribly wrong about the great. Emile Zola is here terribly wrong about Baudelaire, Gertrude Stein about Ezra Pound, Emerson about Jane Austen, Edmund Wilson about W. H. Auden, George Bernard Shaw about Shakespeare, and just about everybody about Walt Whitman. A pleasure, but an intimidating one. Why reveal one's blindnesses in this way? The risks of reviewing are clearly considerable, the rewards minimal. Why do it?

One does it, I suppose, for a number of submerged reasons that don't look particularly attractive in the light. One of them, obviously, is that it gives one a sense of power to pass judgment on the works of others and become an arbiter of taste. Another is the satisfaction of being clever at someone else's expense. "Writers," notes Saul Bellow, "seldom wish other writers well." Indeed it is a long tradition to take one's fellows amusingly apart in public. Aristophanes did it to his fellow dramatists, Alexander Pope to his fellow poets. In late Medieval times the tradition was formalized in the verse fliting, a war of words, poet against poet, may the most outrageous insults win. The impulse remains the same; now we are merely more indirect. We write reviews.

Not that all reviews are rotten. Far from it. In fact, when the reviewing of books first became common practice in the United States, in the 1840s, it was quite rare to find a rotten review of any book, however egregious a production it may have been. We must not assume, however, that this was some golden age of concord between authors and Reviewers. The concord was entirely between publishers and newspapers, the former paying the latter, by one quiet means or another, for favorable reviews.

The system fell apart in 1855 when an anonymous Reviewer for the *Boston Daily Evening Traveller* called Longfellow's *Hiawatha* "childish nonsense" and regretted that our "pet national poet" could find no better subject for his muse "than the silly legends of the savage aborigines." This so outraged Longfellow's publisher, James T. Fields, that he wrote the *Traveller* and indignantly removed all his advertising from the paper. The *Traveller* promptly printed Fields' letter under the title, "Attempt to Coerce the Press." A few weeks later a publisher's newsletter attacked the *Traveller* and defended Fields, admitting in the process that if publishers "seek to bribe the press . . . it is from necessity, not choice." For the press, according to the publishers, demanded to be bribed. " 'Give us advertisements and we will give good notices' is a proposition made every day to publishers," said the publishers. With the fat now in the fire there was no way to avoid a general conflagration. Several eminent Reviewers were discovered to be salaried employees of the publishers whose books they were reviewing. Some publishers had been helpfully sending to newspapers along with their books unsigned reviews that they themselves had written, with the helpful hint that the papers were free to use these reviews however they wished. It was all terribly scandalous and it had to stop.

Some publishers, I'm sure, still think there should be no rotten reviews. Some writers think so, too. Kurt Vonnegut is known to believe that no one should review fiction badly. Anthony Burgess said recently in *TLS* (replying at length to a rotten review of one of his own books) that "In my capacity as critic I never stab anybody, for I know how life-denying it is to be stabbed. Writing a book is damned difficult work, and you ought to praise any book if you can." Burgess was sufficiently worldly to add, however, that "praise is a bland commodity and readers don't like to read it." Indeed. No one would publish an anthology of wonderful reviews of worthless authors, plentiful as they are; no, we get only devilish entertainments like this. Which is another reason why Reviewers do it. They have their public, too; they know what that public demands. And the public must be served.

Not that Reviewers earn much respect for their work, even from the public they try so hard to satisfy. Even, at times, from themselves. "We are generally a poor lot," wrote the sometime Reviewer Leslie Stephen to his friend Thomas Hardy, "horribly afraid of not being in the fashion, and disposed to give ourselves airs on very small grounds." Evidence exists that Reviewers have only a small impact on the sale of books; a study in West Germany some years ago indicated that word-of-mouth sold books at twice the rate of reviews. Certainly bad reviews are no restraint on the sale of James Michener's books, as they were not on those of Jacqueline Susann's, or Frances Parkinson Keyes', or Susan Warner's. (Who were these people? you ask. *Sic transit gloria mundi*.) This does not prevent authors from hating Reviewers and taking their revenge as only they know how. It is well known what Pope did to Colley Cibber in the *Dunciad*. Byron wrote a whole poem satirizing Scotch Reviewers, and it made him famous. The eminent writer I reviewed took her revenge on me, writing a scathing letter to the publication my Review appeared in indicating that I had no sense of humor. Naturally the publication printed it.

All of this has a serious side, as the rage of my particular Reviewee attests. Rotten reviews hurt, for one thing. And if they don't, perhaps, affect sales, they do affect literary reputations, which, as most authors will agree, are more important than sales in the end. This anthology would seem to demonstrate that ultimately it doesn't matter; the good will drive out the bad, Melville endures while the Reviewers who made his life a torment are long forgotten. Perhaps. But how many great talents have been rendered mute and inglorious because, early on, Reviewers accused them of "sophistry," or of attacking "the most sacred associations of life," or of being "dangerous"? These were some of the milder epithets levelled at Melville. The man stopped writing, remember, for nearly forty years.

But now he has his revenge, and we his readers can take our vicarious pleasure in it. We have all, writers and non-writers alike, received bad notices of one sort or another. Our bosses criticize our work, our wives or our husbands walk out on us, our children wonder out loud how on earth we ever made it to adulthood. A friend of mine has on his refrigerator a sign that reads, "Avenge yourself. Live long enough to become a problem to your children." Write well enough that someday your Reviewers will look like fools. Especially the famous ones, great writers themselves, who turned out to be terribly wrong about you.

That is the chief pleasure of this little book, the vision of history setting things right, the judgment of the ages settling old scores. But it is not necessarily a simple plea-sure. As an occasional Reviewer it behooves me to point out that some of these rotten reviews have a twist to them. When Virginia Woolf declares James Joyce's *Ulysses* a "misfire," we smile, but it is a crooked smile, for how many of us have actually been able to read *Ulysses* all the way through? How many of us have found this or that classic boring and unpalatable? George Eliot observed in her notebook that "a man who dares to say that he finds an eminent classic feeble here, extravagant there, and in general overrated, may chance to give an opinion which has some genuine discrimination in it concerning a new work or a living thinker—an opinion such as can hardly ever be got from the reputed judge who is a correct echo of the most approved phrases con-cerning those who have been already canonized."

It is the new work or the living thinker Reviewers primarily are called upon to judge, and it takes a certain courage on their part to be willing to be wrong. They are a poor lot indeed, ill-paid, despised all around, and often wrong, but they have their pride. Smile, then, but let it be a crooked smile; and ask yourself as you look at these rotten reviews whether you would have had the courage or the insight in 1855, say, to recognize the greatness of the author of *Leaves of Grass* when the rest of the literary world, almost to a man, was calling him a clown.

ANTHONY BRANDT

ROTTEN REVIEWS REDUX

WINESBURG, OHIO
SHERWOOD ANDERSON
1918

We sympathize with Mr. Anderson and with what he is trying to do. He tries to find honest mid-American gods. Yet either he never does quite find them or he can never precisely set forth what he has found. It seems probable that he caricatures even Winesburg, Ohio.

The Nation

ON
MATTHEW ARNOLD

Arnold is a dandy Isaiah, a poet without passion, whose verse, written in surplice, is for freshmen and for gentle maidens who will be wooed to the arms of these future rectors.

George Meredith, *Fortnightly Review*   1909

ON
W.H. AUDEN

Mr. Auden himself has presented the curious case of a poet who writes an original poetic language in the most robust English tradition but who seems to have been arrested in the mentality of an adolescent schoolboy.

Edmund Wilson, *The Shores of Light*   1952

PRIDE
AND PREJUDICE
JANE AUSTEN
1813

Why do you like Miss Austen so very much? I am puzzled on that point ... I should hardly like to live with her ladies and gentlemen, in their elegant but confined houses ... Miss Austen is only shrewd and observant.

Charlotte Brontë, letter to G.H. Lewes   1848

ON
JANE AUSTEN

Mama says that she was then the prettiest, silliest, most affected, husband-hunting butterfly she ever remembers.

Mary Russell Mitford, letter to Sir William Etford   1815

I am at a loss to understand why people hold Miss Austen's novels at so high a rate, which seem to me vulgar in tone, sterile in artistic invention, imprisoned in the wretched conventions of English society, without genius, wit, or knowledge of the world. Never was life so pinched and narrow. The one problem in the mind of the writer ... is marriageableness ... Suicide is more respectable.

Ralph Waldo Emerson, *Journal*   1861

ON
FRANCIS BACON

His faults were—we write it with pain—coldness of heart, and meanness of spirit. He seems to have been incapable of feeling strong affection, of facing great dangers, of making great sacrifices. His desires were set on things below, titles, patronage, the mace, the seals, the coronet, large houses, fair gardens, rich manors, many services of pate . . ."

T.B. Macaulay, *Essays*   1842

ON
HONORÉ DE BALZAC

Little imagination is shown in invention, in the creating of character and plot, or in the delineation of passion . . . M. de Balzac's place in French literature will be neither considerable nor high.

Eugene Poitou, *Revue des Deux Mondes*   1856

THE END OF THE ROAD
JOHN BARTH
1958

The same road that has been travelled with Kerouac and to an extent Herbert Gold, this is for those schooled in the waste matter of the body and the mind; for others, a real recoil.

Kirkus Reviews

LES FLEURS DU MAL
CHARLES BAUDELAIRE
1857

In a hundred years the histories of French literature will only mention (this work) as a curio.

Emile Zola, in *Emile Zola*　1953

MOLLOY; MALONE DIES;
THE UNNAMEABLE
SAMUEL BECKETT
1959
(three novels in one volume)

In attempting to depict the boredom of human existence, he has run the very grave risk of thoroughly boring his reader.

San Francisco Chronicle

The suggestion that something larger is being said about the human predicament . . . won't hold water, any more than Beckett's incontinent heroes can.

The Spectator

ON
MAX BEERBOHM

He is a shallow, affected, self-conscious fribble—so there.

Vita Sackville-West, letter to Harold Nicolson　1959

DANGLING MAN
SAUL BELLOW
1944

As the publishers say, it is a sympathetic and understanding study of a young man struggling with his soul. It might be even more sympathetic if Author Bellow (who is not in the Army) ever seemed to suspect that, as an object of pity, his hero is a pharisaical stinker.

Time

WUTHERING HEIGHTS
EMILY BRONTË
1847

Here all the faults of *Jane Eyre* (by Charlotte Brontë) are magnified a thousand fold, and the only consolation which we have in reflecting upon it is that it will never be generally read.

James Lorimer, *North British Review*

. . . wild, confused, disjointed and improbable . . . the people who make up the drama, which is tragic enough in its consequences, are savages ruder than those who lived before the days of Homer.

The Examiner

THE GOOD EARTH
PEARL BUCK
1931

Since Mrs. Buck does not understand the meaning of the Confucian separation of man's kingdom from that of woman, she is like someone trying to write a story of the European Middle Ages without understanding the rudiments of chivalric standards and the institution of Christianity.

New Republic

ON
LORD BYRON

His versification is so destitute of sustained harmony, many of his thoughts are so strained, his sentiments so unamiable, his misanthropy so gloomy, his libertinism so shameless, his merriment such a grinning of a ghastly smile, that I have always believed his verses would soon rank with forgotten things.

John Quincy Adams, *Memoirs*   1830

THE FALL
ALBERT CAMUS
1957

The style is unattractive if apt, being the oblique and stilted flow of a man working his way round to asking for a loan. There is a good deal of jaded Bohemian rot about the bourgeoisie being worse than professional criminals (are we not all guilty, etc.) and outbursts of cynical anguish about platitudes, e.g. 'don't believe your friends when they ask you to be sincere with them.' One might define stupidity as the state of needing to be told this.

Anthony Quinton, *New Statesman*

ALICE IN WONDERLAND
LEWIS CARROLL
1865

We fancy that any real child might be more puzzled than enchanted by this stiff, overwrought story.

Children's Books

JOURNEY TO THE END OF THE NIGHT
LOUIS FERDINAND CÉLINE
1934

Most readers will find *Journey to The End of The Night* a revolting book; its vision of human life will seem to them a hideous nightmare. It does not carry within itself adequate compensation for the bruising and battering of spirit with which one reads it: there is no purgative effect from all these disgusts. If this is life, then it is better not to live.

J.D. Adams, *New York Times Book Review*

DEATH ON THE
INSTALLMENT PLAN
LOUIS FERDINAND CÉLINE
1938

Its effect is to make sympathy, then to put sympathy to sleep, then to exacerbate the nerves of the reader, until, having decided he has as much as he wants to stomach, he throws the book away.

Times Literary Supplement

ON
CHAUCER

Chaucer, not withstanding the praises bestowed on him, I think obscene and contemptible: he owes his celebrity merely to his antiquity, which he does not deserve so well as Piers Plowman or Thomas Erceldoune.

Lord Byron, *The Works of Lord Byron*   1835

UNCLE VANYA
ANTON CHEKHOV
PERFORMED IN NEW YORK, 1949

If you were to ask me what *Uncle Vanya* is about, I would say about as much as I can take.

Robert Garland, *Journal American*

THE AWAKENING
KATE CHOPIN
1899

That this book is strong and that Miss Chopin has a keen knowledge of certain phases of the feminine will not be denied. But it was not necessary for a writer of so great refinement and poetic grace to enter the overworked field of sex fiction.

Chicago Times-Herald

ON
SAMUEL TAYLOR COLERIDGE

We cannot name one considerable poem of his that is likely to remain upon the thresh-floor of fame ... We fear we shall seem to our children to have been pigmies, indeed, in intellect, since a man as Coleridge would appear great to us!

London Weekly Review   1828

YOUTH *and* HEART OF DARKNESS
JOSEPH CONRAD
1902

It would be useless to pretend that they can be very widely read.

Manchester Guardian

Mark Twain keeps score.

THE DEERSLAYER
JAMES FENIMORE COOPER
1841

In one place in Deerslayer, and in the restricted space of two-thirds of a page, Cooper has scored 114 offences against literary art out of a possible 115. It breaks the record.

Mark Twain, *How to Tell A Story and Other Essays* 1897

THE BRIDGE
HART CRANE
1932

A form of hysteria . . . One thing he has demonstrated, the impossibility of getting anywhere with the Whitmanian inspiration. No writer of comparable ability has struggled with it before and it seems highly unlikely that any writer of comparable genius will struggle with it again.

Yvor Winters, *Poetry*

MAGGIE: A GIRL OF THE STREETS
STEPHEN CRANE
1893

. . . we should classify Mr. Crane as a rather promising writer of the animalistic school. His types are mainly human beings of the order which makes us regret the power of literature to portray them. Not merely are they low, but there is little that is interesting in them.

The Nation

BLEAK HOUSE
CHARLES DICKENS
1853

More than any of its predecessors chargeable with not simply faults, but absolute want of construction ... meagre and melodramatic.

George Brimley, *The Spectator*

A TALE OF TWO CITIES
CHARLES DICKENS
1859

Last winter I forced myself through his *Tale of Two Cities*. It was a sheer dead pull from start to finish. It all seemed so insincere, such a transparent make-believe, a mere piece of acting.

John Burroughs, *Century Magazine* 1897

ON
CHARLES DICKENS

We do not believe in the permanence of his reputation ... Fifty years hence, most of his allusions will be harder to understand than the allusions in *The Dunciad*, and our children will wonder what their ancestors could have meant by putting Mr. Dickens at the head of the novelists of his day.

Saturday Review 1858

ON
EMILY DICKINSON

An eccentric, dreamy, half-educated recluse in an out-of-the-way New England village—or anywhere else—cannot with impunity set at defiance the laws of gravitation and grammar . . . Oblivion lingers in the immediate neighborhood.

Thomas Bailey Aldrich, *Atlantic Monthly* 1892

ON
JOHN DONNE

Of his earlier poems, many are very licentious; the later are chiefly devout. Few are good for much.

Henry Hallam, *Introduction to the Literature of Europe* 1837

THE 42nd PARALLEL
JOHN DOS PASSOS
1930

. . . he is like a man who is trying to run in a dozen directions at once, succeeding thereby merely in standing still and making a noise. Sometimes it is amusing noise and alive; often monotonous.

V.S. Pritchett, *The Spectator*

THE BIG MONEY
JOHN DOS PASSOS
1936

I found the novel tiresome because people never seemed to matter in the least; they would have gone down under any system, so why blame capitalism for their complete and appalling lack of character? Mr. Dos Passos' America seems to me a figment of his own imagination, and I doubt the value of his reportage of our period.

Herschel Bricknell, *Review of Reviews*

AN AMERICAN TRAGEDY
THEODORE DREISER
1925

The commonplaceness of the story is not alleviated in the slightest degree by any glimmer of imaginative insight on the part of the novelist. A skillful writer would be able to arouse an emotional reaction in the reader but at no moment does he leave him otherwise than cold and unresponsive. One feature of the novel stands out above all others—the figure of Clyde Griffiths. If the novel were great, he would be a great character. As it is, he is certainly one of the most despicable creations of humanity that ever emerged from a novelist's brain. Last of all, it may be said without fear of contradiction that Mr. Dreiser is a fearsome manipulator of the English language. His style, if style it may be called, is offensively colloquial, commonplace and vulgar.

Boston Evening Transcript

MIDDLEMARCH
GEORGE ELIOT
1871-72

Middlemarch is a treasure-house of details, but it is an indifferent whole.

Henry James, *Galaxy*

THE WASTE LAND
T.S. ELIOT
1922

Mr. Eliot has shown that he can at moments write real blank verse; but that is all. For the rest he has quoted a great deal, he has parodied and imitated. But the parodies are cheap and the imitations inferior.

New Statesman

. . . it is the finest horses which have the most tender mouths and some unsympathetic tug has sent Mr. Eliot's

Mr. Eliot practices equitation.

gift awry. When he recovers control we shall expect his poetry to have gained in variety and strength from this ambitious experiment.

Times Literary Supplement

THE COCKTAIL PARTY
T.S. ELIOT
PERFORMED AT EDINBURGH FESTIVAL, 1949

The week after—as well as the morning after—I take it to be nothing but a finely acted piece of flapdoodle.

Alan Dent, *News Chronicle*

ON
RALPH WALDO EMERSON

A hoary-headed and toothless baboon.

Thomas Carlyle, *Collected Works*   1871

Belongs to a class of gentlemen with whom we have no patience whatever—the mystics for mysticism's sake . . . The best answer to his twaddle is *cui bono?*—a very little Latin phrase very generally mistranslated and misunderstood—*cui bono?* to whom is it a benefit? If not to Mr. Emerson individually, then surely to no man.

Edgar Allan Poe, in a chapter of autobiography   1842

Poe answers twaddle.

ON
EURIPIDES

A cliché anthologist . . . and maker of ragamuffin manikins.

Aristophanes, *The Thesmophoriazusae*   411 B.C.

LET US NOW PRAISE
FAMOUS MEN
WALKER EVANS   JAMES AGEE
1941

There are many objectionable passages and references. I am sorry not to be able to recommend this book for the subject is an important one.

L.R. Etzkorn, *Library Journal*

THE YOUNG MANHOOD OF
STUDS LONIGAN
JAMES T. FARRELL
1934

Unfortunately the author's interest in attempting to shock his readers appears to be greater than his interest in an accurate characterization of the young men around whom this story is developed.

American Journal of Sociology

A case history, true for this boy Studs Lonigan, but not completely valid as the recreation of a social stratum which it also would seem to aim at being.

New York Times Book Review

AS I LAY DYING
WILLIAM FAULKNER
1930

. . . the critic can hardly be blamed if some categorical imperative which persists in the human condition (even at this late date) compels him to put his book in a high place in an inferior category.

New York Times Book Review

LIGHT IN AUGUST
WILLIAM FAULKNER
1932

Despite Mr. Faulkner's great gifts and deep sensitivity, what he is actually offering us is a flight from reality. It's horrors and obscenities in no way contradict this, for many persons, tired of ordinary life, have been known to seek amusement courting nightmares.

The Bookman

ABSALOM, ABSALOM!
WILLIAM FAULKNER
1936

From the first pages of this novel to the last we are conscious that the author is straining for strangeness. He will say nothing simply. His paragraphs are so long and so involved that it is hard to remember who is talking or the subject which began the paragraph . . . We doubt the story just as we doubt the conclusion . . . We do not doubt the existence of decadence, but we do doubt that it is the most important or the most interesting feature in American life, or even Mississippi life.

Boston Evening Transcript

The final blowup of what was once a remarkable, if minor, talent.

Clifton Fadiman, *The New Yorker*

TOM JONES
HENRY FIELDING
1749

A book seemingly intended to sap the foundation of that morality which it is the duty of parents and all public instructors to inculcate in the minds of young people.

Sir John Hawkins, *Life of Samuel Johnson*   1787

I scarcely know a more corrupt work.

Samuel Johnson, quoted in *Memoirs*, Hannah More   1780

THE GREAT GATSBY
F. SCOTT FITZGERALD
1925

What has never been alive cannot very well go on living. So this is a book of the season only . . .

New York Herald Tribune

A little slack, a little soft, more than a little artificial, *The Great Gatsby* falls into the class of negligible novels.

Springfield Republican

Mr. F. Scott Fitzgerald deserves a good shaking . . . *The Great Gatsby* is an absurd story, whether considered as romance, melodrama, or plain record of New York high life.

Saturday Review of Literature

TENDER IS THE NIGHT
F. SCOTT FITZGERALD
1934

Any second rate English society novelist could have written this story better than F. Scott Fitzgerald though not one could have touched his best chapters. Is it laziness, indifference, a lack of standards, or imperfect education that results in this constant botching of the first rate by American novelists?

Saturday Review of Literature

... none of the characters in this book is made sufficiently measurable at the beginning to give to his later downhill course anything more than mildly pathetic interest.

William Troy, *The Nation*

MADAME BOVARY
GUSTAVE FLAUBERT
1857

Monsieur Flaubert is not a writer.

Le Figaro

A PASSAGE TO INDIA
E.M. FORSTER
1924

Spiritually it is lacking in insight.

Blanche Watson, *The World Tomorrow*

MOSES AND MONOTHEISM
SIGMUND FREUD
1939

This book is poorly written, full of repetitions, replete with borrowings from unbelievers, and spoiled by the author's atheistic bias and his flimsy psycho-analytic fancies.

Catholic World

THE RECOGNITIONS
WILLIAM GADDIS
1955

The main fault of the novel is a complete lack of discipline ... It is a pity that, in his first novel, Gaddis did not have stronger editorial guidance than is apparent in the book, for he can write very well, even though most of the time he just lets his pen run on.

Kirkus Reviews

ON
EDWARD GIBBON

Gibbon's style is detestable; but is not the worst thing about him.

Samuel Taylor Coleridge, *Complete Works*   1853

Freud analyzes his reviewer.

WILHELM MEISTER
JOHANN WOLFGANG VON GOETHE
1829

Sheer nonsense.

Francis Jeffrey, *The Edinburgh Review*

THE RETURN OF THE NATIVE
THOMAS HARDY
1878

We maintain that the primary object of a story is to amuse us, and in the attempt to amuse us Mr. Hardy, in our opinion, breaks down.

Saturday Review

THE SCARLET LETTER
NATHANIEL HAWTHORNE
1850

Why has our author selected such a theme? . . . the nauseous amour of a Puritan pastor, with a frail creature of his charge, whose mind is represented as far more debauched than her body? Is it in short, because a running undertide of filth has become as requisite to a romance, as death in the fifth act of a tragedy? Is the French era actually begun in our literature?

Arthur Cleveland Coxe, *Church Review*

CATCH-22
JOSEPH HELLER
1961

Heller wallows in his own laughter and finally drowns in it. What remains is a debris of sour jokes, stage anger, dirty words, synthetic looniness, and the sort of antic behavior the children fall into when they know they are losing our attention.

Whitey Balliett, *The New Yorker*

There is a difference, after all, between milking a joke (the great gift of the old comedians) and stretching it out till you kill it. Mr. Heller has enough verve not to have to try so hard to be funny.

William Barrett, *Atlantic Monthly*

... it gasps for want of craft and sensibility ... The book is an emotional hodgepodge; no mood is sustained long enough to register for more than a chapter.

New York Times Book Review

THE SUN ALSO RISES
ERNEST HEMINGWAY
1926

His characters are as shallow as the saucers in which they stack their daily emotions, and instead of interpreting his material—or even challenging it—he has been content merely to make a carbon copy of a not particularly significant surface life of Paris.

The Dial

. . . leaves one with the feeling that the people it describes really do not matter; one is left at the end with nothing to digest.

New York Times

FOR WHOM THE BELL TOLLS
ERNEST HEMINGWAY
1940

At a conservative estimate, one million dollars will be spent by American readers for this book. They will get for their money 34 pages of permanent value. These 34 pages tell of a massacre happening in a little Spanish town in the early days of the Civil War . . . Mr. Hemingway: please publish the massacre scene separately, and then forget *For Whom the Bell Tolls*; please leave stories of the Spanish Civil War to Malraux . . .

Commonweal

This book offers not pleasure but mounting pain; as literature it lacks the reserve that steadies genius and that lack not only dims its brilliance but makes it dangerous in its influence.

Catholic World

Hemingway edits for permanent value.

ON
HEMINGWAY

It is of course a commonplace that Hemingway lacks the serene confidence that he is a full-sized man.

Max Eastman, *New Republic*　1933

BRAVE NEW WORLD
ALDOUS HUXLEY
1932

A lugubrious and heavy-handed piece of propaganda.

New York Herald Tribune

. . . a somewhat amusing book; a bright man can do a good deal with two or three simple ideas.

Granville Hicks, *New Republic*

There are no surprises in it; and if he had no surprises to give us why should Mr. Huxley have bothered to turn this essay in indignation into a novel?

New Statesman and Nation

A DOLL'S HOUSE
HENRIK IBSEN

It was as though someone had dramatized the cooking of a Sunday dinner.

Clement Scott, *Sporting and Dramatic News*　1889

GHOSTS
HENRIK IBSEN
PERFORMED 1891, LONDON

The play performed last night is 'simple' enough in plan and purpose, but simple only in the sense of an open drain; of a loathsome sore unbandaged; of a dirty act done publicly.

Daily Telegram

ON
HENRY JAMES

It is becoming painfully evident that Mr. James has written himself out as far as the international novel is concerned, and probably as far as any kind of novel-writing is concerned.

William Morton Payne, *The Dial*   1884

(still to come from James were *The Bostonians*, *The Turn of the Screw*, *The Ambassadors* and others—Ed.)

James' denatured people are only the equivalent in fiction of those egg-faced, black-haired ladies who sit and sit in the Japanese colour-prints . . . These people cleared for artistic treatment never make lusty love, never go to angry war, never shout at an election or perspire at poker.

H.G. Wells, *Boon, The Mind of The Race, The Wild Asses of the Devil, and the Last Trump*   1915

. . . an idiot, and a Boston idiot, to boot, than which there is nothing lower in the world.

H.L. Mencken, *H.L. Mencken: The American Scene* 1965

DICTIONARY
SAMUEL JOHNSON
1755

I can assure the American public that the errors in Johnson's *Dictionary* are ten times as numerous as they suppose; and that the confidence now reposed in its accuracy is the greatest injury to philology that now exists.

Noah Webster, letter 1807

LIVES OF THE ENGLISH POETS
SAMUEL JOHNSON
1779-81

Johnson wrote the lives of the poets and left out the poets.

Elizabeth Barrett Browning, *The Book of the Poets* 1842

ON
SAMUEL JOHNSON

Insolent and loud, vain idol of a scribbling crowd . . . who, cursing flattery, is the tool of every fawning, flattering fool . . . Features so horrid, were it light, would put the devil himself to flight.

Charles Churchill, letter   1765

FROM HERE TO ETERNITY
JAMES JONES
1951

Certainly America has something better to offer the world, along with its arms and its armies, than such a confession of spiritual vacuum as this.

Christian Science Monitor

ULYSSES
JAMES JOYCE
1922

I finished Ulysses and think it is a misfire . . . The book is diffuse. It is brackish. It is pretentious. It is underbred, not only in the obvious but in the literary sense. A first rate writer, I mean, respects writing too much to be tricky.

Virginia Woolf, in her diary

That the book possesses literary importance, except as a tour de force, is hard to believe. If we are to have the literature of mere consciousness there are numerous examples from the later Henry James to Virginia Woolf which import to consciousness a higher intrinsic value and achieve the forms of art.

Springfield Republican reviewing the American edition   1934

A PORTRAIT OF THE ARTIST AS A YOUNG MAN
JAMES JOYCE
1917

. . . as a treatment of Irish politics, society or religion, it is negligible.

Catholic World

FINNEGANS WAKE
JAMES JOYCE
1939

As one tortures one's way through *Finnegans Wake* an impression grows that Joyce has lost his hold on human life. Obsessed by a spaceless and timeless void, he has outrun himself. We begin to feel that his very freedom to say anything has become a compulsion to say nothing.

Alfred Kazin, *New York Herald Tribune*

ON
JOHN KEATS

John Keats's friends, we understand, destined him to the career of medicine, and he was bound apprentice to a worthy apothecary in town . . . It is a better and wiser

Mr. Keats chooses a profession.

thing to be a starved apothecary than a starved poet, so back to the shop, Mr. John, back to plasters, pills, and ointment boxes. But for heavens sake be a little more sparing of extenuatives and soporifics in your practice than you have been in your poetry.

Blackwood's Magazine   August, 1818

ON
RUDYARD KIPLING

I'm sorry, Mr. Kipling, but you just don't know how to use the English language.

San Francisco Examiner, rejection letter to Kipling   1889

DARKNESS AT NOON
ARTHUR KOESTLER
1941

The book is long, drawn out, full of repetitions, and marred throughout by its obscenity and irreligion.

Catholic World

ON
CHARLES LAMB

Charles Lamb I sincerely believe to be in some considerable degree insane. A more pitiful, rickety, gasping, staggering, Tomfool I do not know.

Thomas Carlyle, 1831, in *The Book of Insults*   1978

THE PLUMED SERPENT
D.H. LAWRENCE
1926

. . . if this writing up of a new faith is intended for a message, then it is only a paltry one, with its feathers, its bowls of human blood and its rhetoric.

The Spectator

LADY CHATTERLEY'S LOVER
D.H. LAWRENCE
1928

D. H. Lawrence has a diseased mind. He is obsessed by sex . . . we have no doubt that he will be ostracized by all except the most degenerate coteries in the literary world.

John Bull

MAIN STREET
SINCLAIR LEWIS
1920

It is full of the realism of fact colored by rather laborious and over clever satire. But it has no sustained action, whether as realism or as satire. It is a bulky collection of scenes, types, caricatures, humorous episodes, and facetious turns of phrase; a mine of comedy from which the ore has not been lifted.

The Weekly Review

BABBITT
SINCLAIR LEWIS
1922

As a humorist, Mr. Lewis makes valiant attempts to be funny; he merely succeeds in being silly. In fact it is as yellow a novel as novel can be.

Boston Evening Transcript

UNDER THE VOLCANO
MALCOLM LOWRY
1947

Mr. Lowry is passionately in earnest about what he has to say concerning human hope and defeat, but for all his earnestness he has succeeded only in writing a rather good imitation of an important novel.

The New Yorker

THE NAKED AND THE DEAD
NORMAN MAILER
1948

For the most part, the novel is a transcription of soldiers' talk, lusterless griping and ironed-out obscenities, too detailed and monotonous to have been imaginatively conceived for any larger purpose but too exact and literal to have been merely guessed at . . . This doesn't mean to

Mr. Lowry imitates an important novel.

deny Mailer his achievement. If he has a taste for transcribing banalities, he also has a talent for it.

New Republic

THE ASSISTANT
BERNARD MALAMUD
1957

Despite its occasional spark of humanity and its melancholy humor this is on the whole too grim a picture to have wide appeal.

Kirkus Reviews

BUDDENBROOKS
THOMAS MANN
1921

Very few Americans will take the trouble to read this book to the end. It contains no climaxes, no vivid surprises . . . Interesting as the story may be it is too loosely constructed, and for many readers that will prove a barrier.

Boston Evening Transcript

Nothing but two thick tomes in which the author describes the worthless story of worthless people in worthless chatter.

Eduard Engel, in *The Art of Folly*   1961

OF HUMAN BONDAGE
W. SOMERSET MAUGHAM
1935

Largely a record of sordid realism.

Athenaeum

Its ethics are frankly pagan.

The Independent

MOBY DICK
HERMAN MELVILLE
1851

. . . an ill-compounded mixture of romance and matter of fact . . . Mr. Melville has to thank himself only if his errors and his heroics are flung aside by the general reader as so much trash belonging to the worst school of Bedlam literature—since he seems not so much unable to learn as disdainful of learning the craft of an artist.

Athenaeum

Redburn was a stupid failure, *Mardi* was hopelessly dull, *White Jacket* was worse than either; and, in fact was such a very bad book, that, until the appearance of *Moby Dick* we had set it down as the very ultimatum of *weakness* to which the author could attain. It seems, however, that we were mistaken. In bombast, in caricature, in rhetorical artifice—generally as clumsy as it is ineffectual—and in low attempts at humor, each of his volumes has been an advance upon its predecessors.

Democratic Review

The captain's ravings and those of Mr. Melville are such as would justify a *writ de lunatico* against all parties.

Southern Quarterly Review

. . . a huge dose of hyperbolical slang, maudlin sentimentalism and tragic-comic bubble and squeak.

William Harrison Ainsworth, *New Monthly Magazine*

This sea novel is a singular medley of naval observation, magazine article writing, satiric reflection upon the conventionalisms of civilized life and rhapsody run mad . . .

The Spectator

PARADISE LOST
JOHN MILTON
1667

. . . do you not know that there is not perhaps *one page* in Milton's *Paradise Lost* in which he has not borrowed his imagry from the *scriptures*? I allow and rejoice that

Christ appealed only to the understanding and affections; but I affirm that after reading Isaiah, or St. Paul's *Epistle to The Hebrews*, Homer and Virgil are disgustingly *tame* to me and Milton himself barely tolerable.

Samuel Taylor Coleridge, *Letters*   1796

I could never read ten lines together without stumbling at some Pedantry that tipped me at once out of Paradise, or even Hell, into the schoolroom, worse than either.

Edward Fitzgerald, *Letters*   1876

LYCIDAS
JOHN MILTON
1638

The diction is harsh, the rhymes uncertain, and the numbers unpleasing . . . Its form is that of a pastoral—easy, vulgar and therefore disgusting.

Samuel Johnson, *Lives of The English Poets*   1779

ON
JOHN MILTON

His fame is gone out like a candle in a snuff and his memory will always stink.

William Winstanley, diary   1687

LOLITA
VLADIMIR NABOKOV
1958

That a book like this could be written—published here—sold, presumably over the counters, leaves one questioning the ethical and moral standards . . . there is a place for the exploration of abnormalities that does not lie in the public domain. Any librarian surely will question this for anything but the closed shelves. Any bookseller should be very sure that he knows in advance that he is selling very literate pornography.

Kirkus Reviews

MCTEAGUE
FRANK NORRIS
1899

. . . grossness for the sake of grossness . . . the world will not be proud of it in that distant tomorrow which irrevocably sets the true value on books of today.

The Literary World

WISE BLOOD
FLANNERY O'CONNOR
1952

A gloomy tale. The author tries to lighten it with humor, but unfortunately her idea of humor is almost exclusively variations on the pratfall . . . Neither satire nor humor is achieved.

Saturday Review of Literature

THE VIOLENT BEAR IT AWAY
FLANNERY O'CONNOR
1960

As a specialist in Southern horror stories, Miss O'Connor's attitude has been wry, her preferences perverse, her audience special.

Kirkus Reviews

APPOINTMENT IN SAMARRA
JOHN O'HARA
1934

There is a thorough-going vulgarity in this book, characteristic of its class, which is a symptom of a lack of knowledge of the novelist's real art . . . I mean an insufferable vulgarity, which has crept into so many of our supposedly advanced novels that someone not squeamish, not unread in earlier literatures, must protest against what is cheapening American fiction . . . What has happened to these young Americans? Do they think that living in a country the most vigorous, the most complex, the most problematical, the most interesting bar none in the world, we are going to be content with sour pap like this? And the tragedy is that they are clever; if they could see, they could write.

H.S. Canby, *Saturday Review of Literature*

MOURNING BECOMES ELECTRA
EUGENE O'NEILL
PERFORMED IN LONDON, 1961

Mourning Becomes Electra is hollow.

Bernard Levin, *Daily Express*

COMMON SENSE
THOMAS PAINE
1776

Shallow, violent and scurrilous.

William Edward Hartpole Lecky, *A History of England in the 18th Century* 1882

THE MOVIEGOER
WALKER PERCY
1961

Mr. Percy's prose needs oil and a good checkup.

The New Yorker

The New Yorker *repairs Mr. Percy's prose.*

THE BIRTHDAY PARTY
HAROLD PINTER

What all this means only Mr. Pinter knows, for as his characters speak in non sequiturs, half-gibberish and lunatic ravings, they are unable to explain their actions, thoughts or feelings. If the author can forget Beckett, Ionesco and Simpson he may do much better next time.

Manchester Guardian   1958

ON
EDGAR ALLAN POE

After reading some of Poe's stories one feels a kind of shock to one's modesty. We require some kind of spiritual ablution to cleanse our minds of his disgusting images.

Leslie Stephen, *Hours in A Library*   1874

A verbal poet merely; empty of thought, empty of sympathy, empty of love for any real thing . . . he was not human and manly.

John Burroughs, *The Dial*   1893

ON
EZRA POUND

A village explainer, excellent if you were a village, but if you were not, not.

Gertrude Stein, in *Dictionary of Biographical Quotation*   1978

REMEMBRANCE OF THINGS PAST
MARCEL PROUST
1913-1928

The sense of effort lies heavy over the whole work. That the book has greatness and passages of beauty redeeming its ugliness none will deny. But the mind demands of literature something that it can approve as well as something that it can enjoy; and in 'Cities of the Plain,' so full of dignitaries, so devoid of dignity, this instinct finds little to satisfy its craving.

> *Saturday Review of Literature* reviewing volume five of *Remembrance of Things Past*

My dear fellow, I may perhaps be dead from the neck up, but rack my brains as I may I can't see why a chap should need thirty pages to describe how he turns over in bed before going to sleep.

> Marc Humblot, French editor, rejection letter to Proust   1912

CALL IT SLEEP
HENRY ROTH
1935

The book lays all possible stress on the nastiness of the human animal. It is the fashion, and we must make the best of the spectacle of a fine book deliberately and as it were doggedly smeared with verbal filthiness.

> *New York Times Book Review*

M. Humblot contemplates turning over.

THE CATCHER IN THE RYE
J.D. SALINGER
1951

Recent war novels have accustomed us all to ugly words and images, but from the mouths of the very young and protected they sound peculiarly offensive . . . the ear refuses to believe.

New York Herald Tribune Book Review

THE HUMAN COMEDY
WILLIAM SAROYAN
1943

Alas! Interested though one is in the attempt, it remains to say that the result is not very happy . . . there is scarcely a trace of Saroyan's characteristic charm of manner, and indeed his art of inspired artlessness now falls extremely flat. This, in short, is an excessively simple and very, very sentimental little concoction.

Times Literary Supplement

KING LEAR
WILLIAM SHAKESPEARE
1605

This drama is chargeable with considerable imperfections.

Joseph Warton, *The Adventurer* 1754

HAMLET
WILLIAM SHAKESPEARE
1601

It is a vulgar and barbarous drama, which would not be tolerated by the vilest populace of France, or Italy . . . one would imagine this piece to be the work of a drunken savage.

Voltaire, (1768), in *The Works of M. de Voltaire* 1901

OTHELLO
WILLIAM SHAKESPEARE
1604

Pure melodrama. There is not a touch of characterization that goes below the skin.

George Bernard Shaw, *Saturday Review* 1897

ANTONY AND CLEOPATRA
WILLIAM SHAKESPEARE
1606

To say that there is plenty of bogus characterization in it . . . is merely to say that it is by Shakespeare.

George Bernard Shaw, *Saturday Review* 1897

JULIUS CAESAR
WILLIAM SHAKESPEARE
PERFORMED IN LONDON, 1898

There is not a single sentence uttered by Shakespeare's Julius Caesar that is, I will not say worthy of him, but worthy of an average Tammany boss.

George Bernard Shaw, *Saturday Review*

ROMEO AND JULIET
WILLIAM SHAKESPEARE
PERFORMED IN LONDON, 1662

March 1st—To the Opera and there saw Romeo and Juliet, the first time it was ever acted; but it is a play of itself the worst that ever I heard in my life, and the worst acted that ever I saw these people do. . . .

Samuel Pepys, *Diary*

A MIDSUMMER NIGHT'S DREAM
WILLIAM SHAKESPEARE
PERFORMED IN LONDON, 1662

The most insipid, ridiculous play that I ever saw in my life.

Samuel Pepys, *Diary*

ON
WILLIAM SHAKESPEARE

Shakespeare's name, you may depend on it, stands absurdly too high and will go down. He had no invention as to stories, none whatever. He took all his plots from old novels, and threw their stories into a dramatic shape, at as little expense of thought as you or I could turn his plays back again into prose tales.

Lord Byron, letter to James Hogg   1814

ARMS AND THE MAN
GEORGE BERNARD SHAW
PERFORMED IN LONDON, 1894

Shaw may one day write a serious and even an artistic play, if he will only repress his irreverent whimsicality, try to clothe his character conceptions in flesh and blood, and realize the difference between knowingness and knowledge.

William Archer, *World*

MAJOR BARBARA
GEORGE BERNARD SHAW
PERFORMED IN LONDON, 1905

There are no human beings in *Major Barbara:* only animated points of view.

William Archer, *World*

MAN AND SUPERMAN
GEORGE BERNARD SHAW
PERFORMED IN LONDON, 1904

I think Shaw, on the whole, is more bounder than genius ... I couldn't get on with *Man and Superman:* it disgusted me.

Bertrand Russell, letter to G.L. Dickinson

PROMETHEUS UNBOUND
PERCY BYSSHE SHELLEY
1819

... absolute raving ... his principles are ludicrously wicked, and his poetry a melange of nonsense, cockneyism, poverty and pedantry.

Literary Gazette

THE JUNGLE
UPTON SINCLAIR
1906

His reasoning is so false, his disregard of human nature so naive, his statement of facts so biased, his conclusions so perverted, that the effect can be only to disgust many honest, sensible folk with the very terms he uses so glibly.

The Bookman

THE FAERIE QUEENE
EDMUND SPENSER
1590-96

The tediousness of continued allegory, and that too seldom striking or ingenious, has also contributed to render the Fairy Queen peculiarly tiresome ... Spenser maintains his place upon the shelves, among our English classics; but he is seldom seen on the table.

David Hume, in *The History of Great Britain*   1759

ON
GERTRUDE STEIN

It's a shame you never knew her before she went to pot. You know a funny thing, she never could write dialogue. It was terrible. She learned how to do it from my stuff ... She never could forgive learning that and she was afraid people would notice it, where she'd learned it, so she had to attack me. It's a funny racket, really. But I swear she was damned nice before she got ambitious.

Ernest Hemingway, in *Green Hills of Africa*   1935

OF MICE AND MEN
JOHN STEINBECK
1937

An oxymoronic combination of the tough and tender, *Of Mice and Men* will appeal to sentimental cynics, cyn-

Mr. Hume struck by an allegory.

ical sentimentalists . . . Readers less easily thrown off
their trolley will still prefer Hans Andersen.

Time

LIE DOWN IN
DARKNESS
WILLIAM STYRON
1951

What is evident in this first novel is an eagerness and a
sincerity which ought to have been served by an able and
understanding editor. Mr. Styron however had no Max-
well Perkins to guide him, with the result that he has
written here a serious work of fiction which should not
have exceeded 300 pages in length, and which need not
have been done in so turgid and often confused a manner
. . . Mr. Styron leaves his readers curiously unsympathetic.

August Perleth, *Chicago Tribune*

GULLIVER'S TRAVELS
JONATHAN SWIFT
1726

. . . evidence of a diseased mind and lacerated heart.

John Dunlop, *The History of Fiction*   1814

A counsel of despair.

George A. Aitken, *Gulliver's Travels*   1896

WALDEN
HENRY DAVID THOREAU
1854

I look upon a great deal of the modern sentimentalism about Nature as a mark of disease. It is one more symptom of the general liver complaint . . . (Thoreau's) shanty life was a mere impossibility so far as his own conception of it goes, as an entire independency of mankind. He squatted on another man's land; he borrows his axe; his boards, his nails, his fish hooks, his plough, his hoe— all turn state's evidence against him as an accomplice in the sin of that artificial civilization which rendered it possible that such a person as Henry David Thoreau should exist at all.

James Russell Lowell, 1865, from *Literary Essays*   1890

ANNA KARENINA
LEO TOLSTOI
1877

Sentimental rubbish . . . Show me one page that contains an idea.

The Odessa Courier

THE ADVENTURES OF
HUCKLEBERRY FINN
MARK TWAIN
1884

A gross trifling with every fine feeling . . . Mr. Clemens has no reliable sense of propriety.

Springfield Republican

ON
MARK TWAIN

A hundred years from now it is very likely that 'The Jumping Frog' alone will be remembered.

Harry Thurston Peck, *The Bookman*   1901

RABBIT RUN
JOHN UPDIKE
1960

This grim little story is told with all the art we have learned to expect from Updike, but the nagging question remains: what does it come to? Rabbit, Janice and Ruth are all creatures of instinct, floundering in a world they cannot understand . . . The author fails to convince us that his puppets are interesting in themselves or that their plight has implications that transcend their narrow world.

Milton Crane, *Chicago Tribune*

CANDIDE
VOLTAIRE
1759

It seems to have been written by a creature of a nature wholly different from our own, indifferent to our lot, rejoicing in our sufferings, and laughing like a demon or an ape at the misery of this human race with which he has nothing in common.

Mme de Staël, *De L'Allemagne*

ALL THE KING'S MEN
ROBERT PENN WARREN
1946

Somewhere, Mr. Warren loses his grip on his backwoods opportunities and becomes so absorbed in a number of other characters that what might have been a useful study of an irresponsible politician whose prototype we have had melancholy occasion to observe in the flesh turns out to be a disappointment.

The New Yorker

The language of both men and women is coarse, blasphemous and revolting—their actions would shame a pagan hottentot.

Catholic World

VILE BODIES
EVELYN WAUGH
1930

Mr. Waugh displays none of the élan that distinguishes the true satirist from the caricaturist. For all its brilliance the writing lacks vitality. The invention is tired, and effects are too often got by recourse to the devices of slapstick exaggeration.

Dudley Fitts, *The Nation*

MISS LONELYHEARTS
NATHANAEL WEST
1933

A knowledge of its contents will be essential to conversational poise in contemporary literature during the next three months—perhaps.

Boston Evening Transcript

LEAVES OF GRASS
WALT WHITMAN
1855

No, no, this kind of thing won't do . . . The good folks down below (I mean posterity) will have none of it.

James Russell Lowell, quoted in *The Complete Works*, Vol. 14   1904

Whitman is as unacquainted with art as a hog is with mathematics.

The London Critic

Of course, to call it poetry, in any sense, would be mere abuse of language.

William Allingham, letter to W.M. Rossetti   1857

DRUM-TAPS
WALT WHITMAN
1865

Mr. Whitman's attitude seems monstrous. It is monstrous because it pretends to persuade the soul while it slights the intellect; because it pretends to gratify the feelings while it outrages the taste . . . Our hearts are often touched through a compromise with the artistic sense but never in direct violation of it.

Henry James, *The Nation*

ON
WALT WHITMAN

Incapable of true poetical originality, Whitman had the cleverness to invent a literary trick, and the shrewdness to stick to it.

Peter Bayne, *Contemporary Review*   1875

Whitman instructs hog.

Whitman, like a large shaggy dog, just unchained, scouring the beaches of the world and baying at the moon.

Robert Louis Stevenson, *Familiar Studies*   1882

... his lack of a sense of poetic fitness, his failure to understand the business of a poet, is clearly astounding.

Francis Fisher Browne, *The Dial*   1882

He was a vagabond, a reprobate, and his poems contain outbursts of erotomania so artlessly shameless that their parallel in literature could hardly be found with the author's name attached. For his fame he has to thank just those bestially sensual pieces which first drew him to the attention of all the pruriency of America. He is morally insane, and incapable of distinguishing between good and evil, virtue and crime.

Max Nordau, *Degeneration*   1895

THE PICTURE OF
DORIAN GRAY
OSCAR WILDE
1891

... unmanly, sickening, vicious (though not exactly what is called 'improper'), and tedious.

Athenaeum

LOOK HOMEWARD, ANGEL
THOMAS WOLFE
1929

It seems to be the great gift of Mr. Wolfe that everything is interesting, valuable, and significant to him. It must be confessed that he has just missed the greatest of gifts, that of being able to convey his interest to the ordinary reader.

Basil Davenport, *Saturday Review of Literature*

TO THE LIGHTHOUSE
VIRGINIA WOOLF
1927

Her work is poetry; it must be judged as poetry, and all the weaknesses of poetry are inherent in it.

New York Evening Post

THE WAVES
VIRGINIA WOOLF
1931

This chamber music, this closet fiction, is executed behind too firmly closed windows . . . The book is dull.

H.C. Harwood, *Saturday Review of Literature*

THE PRELUDE
WILLIAM WORDSWORTH
1850

The story is the old story. There are the old raptures about mountains and cataracts. The old flimsy philosophy about the effect of scenery on the mind; the old crazy mystical metaphysics; the endless wilderness of dull, flat, prosaic twaddle . . ."

T.B. Macaulay, in his journal

NATIVE SON
RICHARD WRIGHT
1940

The astounding thing is that the publisher is able to send out with the book a typescript about the weight of a Tor Bay Sole entirely made up of favorable reviews from the American Press. Over here and away from that particular racial problem the book seems unimpressive and silly, not even as much fun as a thriller.

New Statesman and Nation

FURTHER THOUGHTS ON THE ART OF
REVIEWING

FURTHER THOUGHTS ON THE ART OF REVIEWING

When a man publishes a book, there are so many stupid things said that he declares he'll never do it again. The praise is almost always worse than the criticism.

SHERWOOD ANDERSON

I have long felt that any reviewer who expresses rage and loathing for a novel is preposterous. He or she is like a person who has just put on full armor and attacked a hot fudge sundae or banana split.

KURT VONNEGUT, JR.

It's surprising that authors should expect kindness to be shown to their books when they are not themselves known for kindness toward their characters, their culture or by implication their readers.

ANATOLE BROYARD

A person who publishes a book willfully appears before the populace with his pants down ... If it is a good book nothing can hurt him. If it is a bad book, nothing can help him.

EDNA ST. VINCENT MILLAY

FURTHER THOUGHTS ON THE ART OF
REVIEWING

A unanimous chorus of approval is not an assurance of survival; authors who please everyone at once are quickly exhausted.

ANDRÉ GIDÉ

. . . reviewers do not read books with much care . . . their profession is more given to stupidity and malice and literary ignorance even than the profession of novelist.

ANTHONY BURGESS

Some reviews give pain. This is regrettable, but no author has the right to whine. He was not obliged to be an author. He invited publicity, and he must take the publicity that comes along.

E.M. FORSTER

It is advantageous to an author that his book should be attacked as well as praised. Fame is a shuttlecock. If it be struck at one end of the room, it will soon fall to the ground. To keep it up, it must be struck at both ends.

SAMUEL JOHNSON

Nature fits all her children with something to do,
He who would write and can't write, can surely review.

JAMES RUSSELL LOWELL

FURTHER THOUGHTS ON THE ART OF REVIEWING

Confronted by an absolutely infuriating review it is sometimes helpful for the victim to do a little personal research on the critic. Is there any truth to the rumor that he had no formal education beyond the age of eleven? In any event, is he able to construct a simple English sentence? Do his participles dangle? When moved to lyricism does he write "I had a fun time"? Was he ever arrested for burglary? I don't know that you will prove anything this way, but it is perfectly harmless and quite soothing.

JEAN KERR

PUSHCART